Copyright © 2021

Poems © Jordan Trethewey 2021

Artwork © Marcel Herms 2021

Layout: Pski's Porch

All rights reserved. No part of this book may be reproduced in any form by any electronic or mechanical means including photocopying, recording, or information storage and retrieval without permission in writing from the author.

ISBN-13: 978-1-948920-24-7
ISBN-10: 1-948920-24-7
for more books, visit Pski's Porch:
www.pskisporch.com

Printed in U.S.A.

Unexpected Mergers

Jordan Trethewey

and Marcel Herms

Praise for *Unexpected Mergers*

Jordan Trethewey gets it right. His collaborations with Marcel Herms are truly, as the title declares, Unexpected Mergers. This is Trethewey and Herms' second collaboration in three years, and like 2019's *Spirits For Sale*, the tone is dark, creepy, dare I say Goth, and highly imaginative. As a writer who is comfortable working with artists, Trethewey's words do more than respond to the images; they inhabit them. Looking through and reading *Unexpected Mergers* becomes a chicken and the egg proposition: what came first, the image or the text? While there is a Goth sensibility to the entire book, there is also an underlying lyrical wit that transforms the readers' experience to one of, if not joy, then pleasure. This is a book that has to be seen to be believed, so take a dive into the strange world of Trethewey and Herms; you'll relish the experience.

— Danny Shot, author of *Works*, and head poetry editor at Red Fez

Like all good ekphrastic works, Jordan Trethewey's poems and Marcel Herms' artwork could successfully stand alone, yet side-by-side in Unexpected Mergers they transmute. They both reflect one another and flavor each other's narratives. With saturated color and playful language—"you just tickled/the pickled and powdered/plastered grins they contain"—the works toggle between darkness and light, death and living—"nature will provide until/we finish poisoning it/so let's just go downtown/have an expensive drink." The paintings suggest human forms, yet with undefined borders, trailing off into their tinted and textured milieu. In the same way the poems eschew traditional punctuation and capitalization—lessening the text's boundaries on the page. Words and art shape mini-stories which touch on normalcy yet refuse to linger there—just concrete enough to weigh them to earth and avoid floating off into dreamlike obscurity. "It's not uncomfortable/just unfamiliar."

— Kerry Trautman, author of *To Have Hoped, Artifacts,* and *To Be Nonchalantly Alive*

Jordan Trethewey and Marcel Herms merge the literary and the visual, enhancing both parts, transforming them into a single state. Jordan's narratives vocalize each piece, allowing us to see and read layers of intent and meaning in Marcel's dynamic paintings.

It was a joy to be involved early on with the digital layout of these mergers, allowing me a very close look at each work. I recommend this close view to everyone.

— Jenn Zed, visual artist, musician, poet

For Jenn Zed—collaborator, critic, compatriot, friend.

Contents

Foreword 1
dead people are more friendly than live ones 5
It's a rich man's game, no matter what they call it 7
In bloom at the port of souls 9
Stuck in this room without a door 11
Leave me alone so I can rock again. 13
Your hills are on fire, why don't you go downtown 15
in search of the magic mushroom 17
Trying to keep the demons outside 19
The trouble I've seen 21
We're in this together now, ... 23
Sometimes I feel like pourin' it all out— 25
No direction home 27
an unacceptable situation. 29
A day at the beach 31
Drama Queen Blues. 33
Daily Bread. 35
Junk sculpture turning back into junk 37
Wegwezen! or Every Relationship 39
I need a private world. 41
the talkin' mob 43
Nobody's Town. 45
Hey boy, I can see you are one of our own 47
He's a fat little insect. 49
It's okay (we love you anyway). 51
When the bones of your nightmares
shine through your skin 53
keep playing that rock & roll. 55

There are worse things than being alone 57
Nothing here but the smell of empty years 59
Climb on your car of fire and leave the country 61
Just spit it back 63
I want to be mixed away 65
Long time man 67
Through Night Windows 69
A Return 71
Reprobate Blues 73
Boys don't cry 75
And he never came back 77
Nerves Shot 79
Too Busy to Live 81
The contact is difficult 83

Foreword

One Summer night in 2018, I went to the Emergency Room at my local hospital with severe abdominal pain. Twenty-four hours later I was diagnosed with acute appendicitis and prepped for surgery. In a recovery room, after the morphine wore off, I picked up my phone to scroll through the image gallery of a contemporary Dutch painter named Marcel Herms.

I recently discovered Marcel's work through the world of online art forums, and was struck by his unique Art Brut style. I began reading the titles of his mixed media paintings, and immediately drew connections among the words, images, and my life's lens. If I remember correctly (forgive me, I was tired and in a narcotic haze), I wrote the first two ekphrastic pieces on my phone while still in an uncomfortable hospital bed: "dead people are more friendly than live ones," and "It's a rich man's game, no matter what they call it."

I immediately messaged them to Marcel in Deventer, Netherlands. He was enthusiastic and encouraged me to continue. I wrote 33 more in a matter of months, enjoying the spontaneous creative process. After publishing my second collaboration with Marcel (and first with Pski's Porch) in 2019 called, "Spirits for Sale," I returned to this first collaboration and wrote five more pieces inspired by new Marcel images, bringing the total to an even 40.

The Muses set me inside a hypnotic and intense creative groove, nurtured by Marcel's artistic vision, encouragement, and spirit of exploration. Experiences like this are as rare as winning the lottery. Thanks, Marcel.

Unexpected Mergers

dead people are more friendly than live ones

i arrived home
only bleached bones
for an audience
to relate my story
of the far-off people
who protected me
while my own
no longer could

It's a rich man's game, no matter what they call it

step right up
your charity
is our business
join the solution
don't be a cause
take the pistol
aim the stream
at the dehydrated
orphan's cracked lips
every little bit helps
watch your hard-earned
tokens disappear in my palm
maintaining the illusion

In bloom at the port of souls

Dad became a long-haul, roadside statistic.
Mother's heart failed at the news.

Neurotic Nell's separation anxiety
caused her to keel over by the back door

when neither returned—left only with me
arriving twice-a-day to feed her.

All returned to earthly ash,
I dug a ring around the rosies,

shook their condensed nutrients inside
like confetti at a worm wedding.

Outside my picture window,
their muted colours return

brilliant each Spring
in bloom.

Stuck in this room without a door

yet not afraid or alone
with an endless quantity—
bottles, amber, green, clear,
orange you just tickled
the pickled and the powdered
plastered grins they contain
open other access panels
to straight weekday rituals
and family fracas

a room softly lit
by pharmaceutical effects,
occasionally accented with
distilled and fermented fantasies,
properly validated via exterior
ventilation provides a manageable,
navigable four-walled vista

Leave me alone so I can rock again

It's been five long years
since my red solo cup runneth
over with dirty club draft
and good soul cheer while
deliberately subjecting myself
to unscientific therapeutic tests
using chest-vibrating decibels.

I now wear my foam ear
plugs to damp down
your incessant ego-centric yelps
for attention when I dare
leave your sight lines.

The times I get wet and dirty
in a communal environment
rarely include a soundtrack—
giving tantrum toddlers baths,
witnessing spaghetti nights,
cleaning up deposits from derrières—
but no one in their right mind
would call that a festival.

Your hills are on fire, why don't you go downtown

see what all the fuss is about
you've been cutting firewood
living in a particle board tarpaper
bunkhouse hiding behind
an ancient white pine
when nature truly calls

worlds did collide where
you should have expected it
firewood
           wood
                    fire
and there you stand
in disbelief despite a cigarette
dangling from your lips
a pack of matches
in your callused hand

we worried when you wobbled
backwards on the progress ladder
feigning self-assuredness
while stumbling out the door
embracing fresh air simplicity
solitude in unrefined resourcefulness

take it as a sign given seekers
in old books there is nothing
to be found
you are your own mountain
to climb conquer or quit on
nature will provide until
we finish poisoning it
so let's just go downtown
have an expensive drink

in search of the magic mushroom

only points us nose-deep
in never-ending bogs
of decay and animal plop

searching ambiguous meadows
for gilled silly psilocybin
in dark un-humourous humus

four hours and still no pleasant
disorienting synesthesia,
only angry-red clouding my vision

from pulsating saddle sores
we decide to levitate—
flap our feathered hair

grin our ruthless smiles
clutching four-legged beasts in our thighs
until they buck free

parachuting to lush safety
of bouncy castle fields below
shitting themselves on soft impact

where it spreads like ground hazelnuts
fertilizing another hide-and-seek crop
of organic chemical wonder

Trying to keep the demons outside

is easier said than done.
Every five minutes
they keep pounding on the door
whining and pleading
to be let back in.

We're bored!
It's too cold!
There is too much beauty in nature!
Abbadon broke my toy!
Kitsune tricked me!
Tezrian is picking fights!
Mammon took my money!
Agramon is scaring me!

They want the remotes,
joysticks and controllers
lying around the house—
are lost without them.
Each longs to pour itself
back in well-worn grooves,
wipe their dirty hands
on my white sofa,
cover their farts
with grey throw pillows.

The trouble I've seen

                    nobody knows.

You can look at my face
study my posture
and surmise.

I'll assess
your ability
to engage empathy

                    to listen

to focus on information
provided   through eyes
                   not screens.

If I flinch
from   a comforting hand
don't pull back.

It's not uncomfortable
just   unfamiliar.

We're in this together now,

she said, locking eyes
while I wheeled her
into the N.I.C.U.

We scoured our hands
harsh pink soap
up to the elbows

banishing bacterial bad guys.
Pulsing, humid Plexiglas cubes
atop rolling kitchen islands

adorn the privacy-curtain-
partitioned walls.
Name quickly coloured

by nurse on construction paper.
Her body clad in diaper
and toque, bum

to an artificial sun.
Tiny tube tucked
through nose, down esophagus.

Together we insert
one hand each through
permitted entrance,

making first contact.
Eyes mirror each other's
self-conscious selves,

return to deep-pink,
resting organism—
establishing Point A to B.

Sometimes I feel like pourin' it all out—

my verbal vomitus—
guts seeping into the cracks
between sidewalk blocks
which absorb more
than my fellow beings
standing nearby.

I yell at the echo
chamber of isolating condos
arranged like circular compounds
of dominoes, end-to-end.
Ever-sprouting, they rise
with their backs to us,
enclosing former public spheres
where we could once smile,
nod, throw a ball, speak
of canine eccentricities
while stooping
to keep the grass clean.

Refine your aerosol aim
on what outside interests—
of profit-through-habitat-density
and gentrification—
have provided for self-expression.
Communicate via canvas—
be it mural, tag,
modern hieroglyphic misted
on the flammable faux concrete.

No direction home

Mario Andretti dreams
behind go cart requests

proficiency with power tools
does not equal mechanical inclination

or welding certification
dad on improvisation hotseat

materialize something sleek
a boy might sit on to speculate

plywood pieces, rusty wagon wheel axle
with handle, screwed to pine board

sister's third-hand stroller wheels
Gorilla-glued into rear-end bore holes

safety first, wear your helmet, son,
it might hurt your earnest pride

should mischievous gravity make the wheels
fly off at 2 km/h, remember the fun

of going downhill will never equal
the tortuous return to the top

an unacceptable situation

don't gaslight me—
hand me your version of the past
I remember

witnessed my own history
made mistakes
learned, accepted

rejected, ignored
you are overly emotional
prone to exaggeration

of every fact
you clothe your argument
in fiction

costume me
in a waxed moustache
and smirk

truth is
I crashed on your rocks
the wick has burnt out

in the dark
with uncertainty
I freeze

A day at the beach

will be relaxing, he said.
Sun evaporating anxieties,

the soothing sound of surf,
salt breeze through untamed hair,

humid ocean air in our lungs.
Now I stand exposed

to the elements
and judgmental eyes.

He swears he didn't know
it was a nude affair.

Regrets the challenge—
calling me a prude.

We burn,
struggling to stay warm.

Both occupied
juggling beach balls.

Drama Queen Blues

Vision is blurry—
two-thirds of my body
pummeled numb on the floor.

If I am not present
to witness her histrionics,
she declaims to walls

incapable of escape.
I submit—must admit
I am hammered stiff,

right between the eyes—
paint yellowing like
her jaundiced lips.

Daily Bread

I stare into his mongrel eyes.
He clutches the beef bone
to an emaciated chest.

Broken thumb—a weak spot
to rip dreams of soup
from his manic clutches.

Scar on left cheek,
proof of sharp rights taken
on tracks bound for trouble.

Broken chicklets in misaligned mouth—
a vertical bar graph
of dumpster alley wins and losses.

One defensive scratch from a ragged nail
might mean my shivering death.
I compliment him on his vintage hat.

Junk sculpture turning back into junk

He confiscates toilet paper and paper towel tubes,
empty yogurt containers, bottle caps and rusty screws,
to a damp basement corner studio where he is free
to achieve a singular, scavenger vision.

His unwritten motto in words: nothing is junk.
Packaging does not remain in trash cans for long.
Adept with duct tape, all disparate parts are joined.
An interpretation of humanity
held together with dollar store adhesive.

Accustomed to constant *riiips*!
family praises each Frankenstein-ian achievement.
Uncomfortable with accolades,
he banishes humanoid births to cobweb corners.
Glue slowly separates from seams—
limbs dangle, rust spreads,
staining punctured-plastic eye sockets.

Mouths droop into screams.
Subconscious continuation—
damp disintegration from neglect.

Wegwezen! or Every Relationship

I'm tired of your bellyaching.
You cramp my style.
I wish you were never born.
Get out of my sight.
I don't want to play your games anymore.

Wait...

Don't go.
I didn't mean it.
I'm sorry.
Please come back.
I need you.

I need a private world

free from every living thing
demanding attention and time.

I'll begin stacking plastic toddler bricks,
securing those few, vulnerable experiences
that first caused my brain to glow.

With interlocking Lego,
I'll wall off ingrained expectations.
Allow time to boil adolescent oil
for when they try to breach.

I'll be the smartest little pig—
not cutting construction corners.
Heat-cured earth and muddy mortar
keep adult Dolos wolves at bay.

the talkin' mob

congregates on corner couches
at every party you attend

it chews apart company
instead of hors d'oeuvre
with clicking tongues
clownish lips and clacking teeth

shredding dignity and self-esteem
to scuttlebutt confetti

yet conscientious in its own way
should it sense you didn't overhear
quite willing to let bodies talk
in Pictionary pantomime.

Nobody's Town

They arrived with engraved tablets
we correctly assumed were new edicts to bear
on slumped soldier shoulders.

The newcomers were confused
by the lack of enthusiasm
exhibited by our resting bitch faces,
evolved to withstand varied disappointment.

After the tablets were translated,
our demeanor remained stoic.
Our leaders used thin, high-output lasers—
endorsed a new deal much like the old one.

It was on this day,
the Augmentors began our betterment—
fine-tuned our integration as drones
for their new honeycomb hive.

This was not mind control,
merely redirection of a shiftless, collective
spirit browbeaten into a daze of false hope
via selfish promises.

Hey boy, I can see you are one of our own

even if you do not.
You are young. Your future
                        in front of you.
Trust me,
childish heads enlarge,
grow grotesque with malformed ideas
gifted down the decades
by misinformed family and friends.
You will embrace them as normal—
your own interpretations.

Mind preoccupied,
body falls out of alignment,
expands with lethargy—
each part indistinct from another.

Layer in social camouflage,
obfuscate all entropy.
Remember—
black is slimming.

He's a fat little insect

a noisy narcissistic nuisance
coddled too long in cocoon
any *thing* can feel important
skittering around bacterium drains

atop shit mountain
the throne remains unchallenged
due to indifference not fear
a vague desire to see him slip up

snap a leg and drown
headfirst in a pipe elbow
once thought conquered
with the best words

It's okay (we love you anyway)

despite a rebellious desire
to seek solace in community
devoted to a higher power

we went our own way
Mama Punk, Dada Alt-Country
committed to an aesthetic

in the face of overwhelming parental pressure
we dug in
wrote manifestos

committed them to memory
curated a life uniform
an unflinching style

we get it
your demure Sunday-patterned sweaters
our blue-green hair and Stetson

accept that we will always disagree
on existential bullet points
but you can return home again

on this unpaved road
to care that transcends
autonomy and theology

When the bones of your nightmares shine through your skin

they are about to be born
monsters set free

to sprout spikes and wings
glowing grimaces of grief

their sluggish steps drawn
to an infinite buffet

of World Series homers
rainbow-trotting unicorns

above buzz cuts and ringlets
they devour sparkling fantasy

replace it with cruel collages
composed of adult anxiety

keep playing that rock & roll

however you hear it
whether with paintbrush
keyboard, chisel or clay

keep playing that rock & roll

vibrate your brain
with a busy, resonant buzz
to avoid overthinking

keep playing that rock & roll

inflate your spirit
like a Pink Floyd prop
unafraid to illustrate

keep playing that rock & roll

don't avoid the crowd-pleasers
once-bitten, twice-shy hearts
need to see their reflections

There are worse things than being alone

imagine life in a cult
thoughts always accompanied

trapped in a romance
communing with its corpse

hard work within a team
contributions undervalued

strained smiles
forever worn for others
never to relax
in wrinkled neutrality

Nothing here but the smell of empty years

which
coincidentally
smell like un-rinsed bottles
of celebration wine

those last dry drops
grow microscopic mold
then rise weightless
spore-dust in sunlight

frozen clocks
delineating wasted exuberance
—time

Climb on your car of fire and leave the country

with the speed of a house ablaze
combustion not only destroys
it births singular species
eucalyptus and lodgepole pine

white-hot pursuit of inexplicable love
leaves melted rubber maps on the road
interpret as either tail-tucked return trail
or reckless rear view arrows
pointing toward cliff's edge

but why occupy the driver seat
if unwilling to feel the flames
hesitation sparks fire-retardant failure

Just spit it back

on the sidewalk
all the frothing words
crowed above your head
and behind your back
before you age with them
go crazy
from negative needling
skipping record repetition
and cut off your ears
hoping clots create
a healing hum
while brushes and blood
spatter your slept-in
Van Gogh smock

I want to be mixed away

in the end
no fear of absence in death
free of consciousness and ego

rub my remains on a canvas
leave fluid streaks
charcoal smudges

twirl my ashes
in bright pools on a palette
darkening the design

forever
in the process
of deconstruction

Long time man

Blood pooled around
clean silhouette
marred by bullet hole
in the head.

Congealing stain
on kitchen tiles—
cause of death evident
without incriminating evidence.

Final drop of love
exsanguinated
the last time he opened
his automatic mouth—

she put a barrel in it.

Through Night Windows

Glancing in windows at night
from sidewalk, I pass by
hoping for narratives lit from inside,
or a decorating idea at least.

A Return

Forget emotional friction.
I want a return

to the physical. I need to
handle, corner your curves,

glide in and out
to mellifluously mid-

tempo bass. Mouths,
hips embraced,

as Tom Waits rasps, "Kiss Me,"
on repeat. Our bodies, in obedience,

re-position
once again.

Reprobate Blues

I got a pocket full of keys, only smile when I sneeze.
The last meal I remember was a block of cheese.
Took it from the grocer when his back was turned.
Five-finger discount; let the coupons burn.

Used to pour molten plastic into molds all day.
Environmentalists came, took my job away.
Checked the Internet for another job.
The only ads were selling stuff to swell your knob.

Well, no benevolent god ever shook my hand
on a deal for a piece of the Promised Land.

Baby kicked me out when we couldn't eat.
I told her she should go, shake her ass down the street.
Now I live under a hedge, and when kids walk by
they laugh and spit at me without wondering why.

Boys don't cry

they rage
anger the easiest emotion
examinations are hard
they won't be coddled
told what to do
if all goes wrong
not their fault
always someone to blame
for poor impulse control

Boys will be boys

they bare teeth
imitation of predators
hiding in glossy textbook
pages they refuse to read
afraid to admit and overcome
what they don't know
haven't considered because
they already know it all

And he never came back

to the town of first
words, first friends,
first love, first
betrayal, first foe.

He couldn't go back.
Stress began to tear
an irreconcilable rift,
leaving him alone

on one side.
An ideological divide grew—
he squinted across
the increasing chasm.

Tremors widened it.
Left no choice,
he stepped into the ash
of crumbling expectations—

one foot, then the next,
hesitant, and free
of the righteous
Richter Scale.

Nerves Shot

Broken teeth and rictus smile,
head shot immortalizes final relief.

Bottle ring stains on hasty hen scratch
attempt to highlight life's lowlights.

A return to thesis unnecessary,
nothing says goodbye like an exit wound.

Too Busy to Live

C'mon! I have to drop you off at martial arts class. Then I need to get to my doctor for my pap test. Nothing to worry about. When I get back, I have to call the plumber—set up a time to see about the foul-smelling water puddling on the basement floor. No worries at all. When I get off the phone with them, I need to call the school, tell them you'll be late tomorrow morning for a dental appointment. Afterward, I'll get the tires out of the shed and put them in the trunk, so I can have them changed at the garage after I drop you off from the dentist. I'm not worried. When I get off the phone, I'll pick up groceries, then swing around to get your sister at rehearsal, and you at karate. Things need to get done. Rooter can do his business when we get back home, you can watch him while I bring the bags in. Then I can get supper started. C'mon! Let's hustle! Are you listening? We gotta go!

The contact is difficult
(Het contact verliep moeizaam)

Words like love,
hugs without trepidation
I packed inside stackable
cardboard compartments,
created the wall hidden
behind since childhood.
Translated heartspeak
to compliant gestures,
perfected responsive loyalty
for those who provided
no emotional frills.
There was a feline gift,
a surrogate listener
that never tried to fix,
yet always understood
the power of another
warm body to soothe.
Now you need more
than a bond expressed
through dutiful deeds.
I can admit
the contact is difficult.
Here is a box cutter—
shorten the blade,
to avoid what's inside.

Jordan Trethewey is a writer and editor living in Fredericton, New Brunswick, Canada. He first joined forces with Pski's Porch Publishing in 2019 with a frightening book of verse, *Spirits for Sale*, available on Amazon. Some of his poetry, fiction, and non-fiction inhabits online publications such as *Burning House Press*, *Visual Verse*, *Carpe Arte Journal*, *Fishbowl Press*, *The Blue Nib*, *Red Fez*, *Anti-Heroin Chic*, *Sheila-Na Gig Editions*, *Drunk Monkeys*, and *Spillwords*. Jordan is an editor at redfez.net, openartsforum.com, and tenmillionflies.com. His poetry is translated in Vietnamese and Farsi. To see more of his work, visit:
jordantretheweywriter.wordpress.com.

Artist Marcel Herms (of the Netherlands) in his studio

Photo © Vincent Nijhof 2017

Marcel Herms is a self-taught artist. His work is about freedom. He never knows what he's going to make before he begins. When Marcel starts a project he tries to accesses his subconscious, and from there, something usually arises. He does not limit himself to one medium, preferring to keep busy with different art forms. Marcel always has music playing while he is working; he feels it provides a freeing atmosphere in which to create. Like music, Marcel's art is about autonomy, licentiousness, passion, color and rhythm.

When Marcel paints he uses everything he can get his hands on: acrylics, oils, inks, pencils, crayons, spray cans, etc. He also mixes paint with sand, sawdust or pieces of paper. He paints on canvas, paper, and other materials, such as wood. He works in different sizes: from very small to very large He creates 3D objects, artist books, audio art, as well as record, CD, and book covers. His work is featured in many national and international publications. He collaborates with numerous visual artists, writers, and audio artists from around the world.

Email: info@MarcelHerms.nl
Website: www.MarcelHerms.nl
Facebook: Marcel Herms and Marcel Herms Art

Pski's Porch Publishing was formed July 2012, to make books for people who like people who like books. We hope we have some small successes. www.pskisporch.com.

323 East Avenue
Lockport, NY 14094
www.pskisporch.com

www.ingramcontent.com/pod-product-compliance
Lightning Source LLC
Chambersburg PA
CBHW042303150426
43196CB00005B/65